Jan wanted some sweets.

Jan went to the sweet shop.

2

The sweet shop was closed.

Jan saw a chocolate machine.

She wanted some chocolate.

Jan put her finger in the machine.

Her finger was stuck.
Jan pulled and pulled.

Jan's mum came.

She couldn't get Jan's finger out.

A man came.

He couldn't get Jan's finger out.

AGENT
P. PATEL
Ice Cream
CLOSED
Telephone

The firemen came.

12

They couldn't get Jan's finger out.

A little boy came.
He put some money in the machine.

14

Out came Jan's finger.

Out came a bar of chocolate.